Dachshund Care

The Complete Guide to Caring for and Keeping Dachshunds as Pets

Canine Care

DestinyGate
Publishing & Distribution

ISBN-13: 978-1537554426

CONTENTS

INTRODUCTION

Before purchasing any pet it is important to understand that as a pet owner you are responsible for the care and wellbeing of your pet. It is important to try and learn as much as you can about the animal you are considering to keep as a pet to make sure that your lifestyle, household and financial status are suited to provide your pet with the best possible care. This guide has been designed to provide you with both precise and concise information about a Dachshund's basic needs to help you provide your pet with the best quality care practices. This guide will give an in-depth explanation on training your Dachshund, raising your dog from a puppy, grooming, health care and everything in between!

DESCRIPTION

The Dachshund (colloquially known as *'The Sausage Dog'*) is a breed of short-legged and long-bodied hound dog. The standard size Dachshund was bred to flush out badgers, and other burrow dwelling animals. In fact the word *'Dachs,'* in German, means 'Badger.' The miniature Dachshund was bred to hunt smaller animals such as rabbits and prairie dogs. Standard sized Dachshunds weigh between 16 and 32 pounds (7 to 14kg) when fully grown. Miniature Dachshunds weigh 11 pounds (5kg) and under. If a Dachshund weighs between 11 and 16 pounds (5 to 7kg), it is referred to as a Tweenie. The breed has three different types of coat: shorthaired, wirehaired and longhaired. Due to their small size, interesting appearance and lively disposition, the Dachshund has become one of the most popular household dog breeds.

Lifespan

Dachshunds commonly live to be between 12 and 14 years old. However it is not uncommon for a Dachshund to live for as long as 15 years, providing they do not develop any serious health issues.

Appearance

A typical Dachshund has a long muscular body and short, stubby legs. The front two paws are normally wide and paddle-shaped to assist with digging. The Dachshund has a deep chest that provides it with increased lung capacity which allows the breed to have increased stamina while hunting prey underground. They have an increased nose area on their snout to allows them to greatly absorb odors, which again assists the breed in hunting underground. Dachshund coats have a wide variety of colors: chocolate, tan, black, cream and red – to name but a few.

Popularity

The Dachshund is a very popular apartment dog due to its small size. They are ranked among the top ten most popular dog breeds in 76 of 190 major US cities! Due to their popularity it will be very easy for you to join an organized local Dachshund club. This will allow you to meet other owners and introduce your dog to other dogs within its breed.

BREED CHARACTERISTICS

The following section will give you a simplistic overview of the characteristics of a Dachshund. Our rating system is from 1 to 10 – with 1 being the lowest score and 10 being the highest.

- **Adaptability:** 6/10
- **Friendliness:** 6/10
- **Health:** 6/10
- **Ease of Grooming:** 7/10
- **Amount of Shedding:** 6/10
- **Trainability:** 8/10
- **Intelligence:** 8/10
- **Exercise Needed:** 6/10
- **Playfulness:** 8/10
- **Family Friendliness:** 10/10

WHY SHOULD YOU PURCHASE A DOG?

In the United States of America it is estimated that there are between 70 and 80 million pet dogs owned and over 40% of the county's households own a dog! As the statistic shows dogs are incredibly popular pets – but why? Any dog owner will happily tell you all the benefits and joys of owning a dog! The following section will outline 5 key benefits of owning a dog:

Companionship

Dogs are incredibly loyal and loving animals and make a great addition to any household. If you build a strong relationship with your pet they can transcend just being a pet and become a friend, or ever a member of your family! However your dog brings you companionship in other ways. You are more likely to interact with strangers while walking your dog than if you were walking alone. Owning a dog also allows you to go to dog parks and converse with other dog owners. If you walk your dog around your neighborhood on a regular basis, you may also develop a friendly relationship with your neighbors who own dogs as you are likely to pass each other several times a day.

Exercise

Owning a dog increases your chance of exercising due to the fact that you will need to play with and walk your dog. Taking your pet for frequent walks will decrease your chance of becoming over weight. A recent study in Australia found that children with a pet dog are 50% less likely to be overweight! Exercising on a regular basis has a plethora of other health benefits such as reducing the chance of heart disease, strokes and high blood pressure. A dog can be a great exercise companion as well as being a great motivation due to the fact that it is cruel to not provide your dog with adequate exercise.

Watchdog

Dogs are very territorial, loyal and aware as a species. Even from as early as puppyhood, a dog is able to detect potential burglars and dangers. Your dog will bark at anything suspicious or out of the ordinary which will alert you to any potential trouble. Most criminals are instantly put off by the barking of a watchdog.

Nurturing

The majority of humans have a deep desire to nurture. This desire used to be fulfilled by caring for, and raising, a baby or caring for younger siblings. Across the Western World the average family size is decreasing which makes pets the perfect outlet for people's nurturing desires. In families with no children, or one child, dogs are fulfilling the role of being substitute children and siblings! Dogs are intelligent beings and respond well to being nurtured which makes it a positive and rewarding experiences for both the owner and the pet. Dogs also seem to nurture children. Children who own a dog tend to have a high self-esteem and are more popular with their classmates!

Empathy

Dogs are incredibly empathetic animals! They will sense the mood of their owner and either attempt to provide comfort, through physical contact, or a distraction through a humorous playful act. It is not uncommon for dogs to bring their distressed owners their favorite toy as an attempt to cheer them up. Dogs have also saved their owners from countless dangers – such as house fires and burglaries.

CHOOSING A BREED

There are hundreds of different dog breeds available for purchase and the importance of choosing a breed that fits your family and lifestyle cannot be overstated! It is more important to consider what your new pet will be like as an adult rather than as a puppy. It is not uncommon for owners to fall in love with the aestheticism of certain breeds while they are puppies but find that the adult dog does not fit their lifestyle. The following section will help you decide which breed is best for you!

Loving Breeds

All breeds of dog can be loving! However the following species have proven themselves to be among the most loving, gentle and affectionate of all breeds: Labrador Retriever, Golden Retriever, Labradoodle, Dalmatian, Cocker Spaniel, English Bulldog, Shih Tzu, Dachshund and Beagle. These breeds are great with children and make fantastic family dogs! Most of the above species are medium to large dogs which means that they are great for small children and toddlers due to the fact that your small child cannot drop, or injure, your dog by mistake.

Guard Dogs

There are plenty of breeds that make fantastic guard dogs. If you would like a breed that is physically intimidating we recommend purchasing a German Shepherd, a Rottweiler, a Doberman Pinscher or a Belgian Malinois. If you just want to purchase a breed that is very territorial, and will bark at strangers, we recommend West Highland Terriers, Yorkshire Terriers and Chihuahuas. Despite not being the most physically intimidating species, these small dog breeds are very noisy and will be sure to deter any potential burglars!

Active Dogs

If you are thinking about purchasing a highly active dog we recommend the following species: Husky, Border Collie, Greyhound, Labrador Retriever, Schnauzer, Jack Russel Terrier and Labradoodle. These species make great exercise partners and will need to be walked multiple times a day. Smaller breeds of dog can be equally as active but will tend to get tired at a faster rate than larger bodied breeds. If you choose a dog that requires a lot of exercise, do not be surprised if it develops destructive behaviors if you do not give it enough exercise.

Silent Dogs

There are a lot of different reasons that you may prefer to purchase a breed that is able to be silent. The following breeds are known to be among the quietest dogs: Beagle, Greyhound, Whippet, English Bulldog, Maltese, Pekingese. It is important to remember that these breeds will still bark but they are dramatically less likely to whine and be yappy. It is also important to remember that puppies tend to be dramatically louder than adult dogs.

Hypoallergenic and Hairless Dogs

No breed of dog is entirely hypoallergenic but there are two types of dog that are less likely to trigger an allergic reaction in people who are sensitive or allergic to dogs and dog hair: hypoallergenic and hairless. Hypoallergenic dog breeds include: Chihuahua, Cockapoo, Greyhound, Havanese, Labradoodle, Border Terrier and Yorkshire Terrier. Hairless dog breeds include: Peruvian Inca Orchid, American Hairless Terrier and the Chinese Crested (the hairless breed).

DOG EQUIPMENT BASICS AND ESSENTIALS

Before purchasing a dog it is important to make sure that you have already purchased all the equipment you will need to provide your new dog with the best possible care. Ensuring you have all the essential equipment before purchasing your pet is the best way to build a strong relationship with your pet and to keep it content, happy and healthy.

Collars and ID Tags

Purchasing a collar with an ID tag is arguably one of the most important things you can purchase for your dog. The collar allows you to attach a leash to your dog, which in turns allows you to take your pet for a walk which is essential to their health. There are a wide range of collars available to purchase made from multiple different materials and styles. It is important to take your dog's habits into account when purchasing a collar. For example if your dog regularly enjoys swimming it is not advisable to purchase a leather collar. It is also important to not purchase a thin collar! When you walk your dog on a leash it may lunge, or pull, which will cause the collar to dig into its neck. The wider the collar is the wider the area the force from the lunge is spread over – basically wider collars are more comfortable! The ID tag allows for your pet to be easily identifiable and returned to you if they are ever lost! We recommend having your dog's name and your home address on the ID tag. This will allow the person who finds your dog to keep it calm by using its familiar name and will know where to return your pet to.

Leashes and Harnesses

Purchasing a lead, or harness, is vital in ensuring your dog remains healthy! Having a lead, or harness, allows for you to walk your pet and provide them with the exercise they need. Walking your pet also helps to create a strong bond and friendship between the two of you. There are a few differences between Leashes and Harnesses which will be explained below:

- **Leash:** Most dog owners will use a leash while walking their pet. Leashes ensure both comfort and safety when you take your dog out for a walk. It is important to buy a leash that extends to allow your dog to explore and move away from you at times. It is equally important to buy a sturdy leash that will allow you to keep control of your pet for the entirety of the walk.
- **Harness:** If you have a large, small, energetic

or boisterous dog a harness may be a safer option. The harness is safer for these types of dogs as they will not feel discomfort from their collar when they pull against the leash. Purchasing a front-clip harness (that goes over the dog's chest) will allow you to have more control over your pet.

Bedding

Some owners allow their dogs to sleep in their beds or on their sofas. While this can definitely be a great way to build a strong relationship with your dog it is also important to purchase a suitable bed for your pet. By providing your pet with its own bed it will give your dog a place of its own to feel safe and secure. There is an overwhelmingly wide variety of dog beds available in pet stores and on the internet. We recommend adhering to the following criteria when purchasing a dog bed to ensure both practicality, safety, comfort and warmth.

- **Natural Materials:** It is important to make sure the dog bed you purchase is made of natural materials. Synthetic products, including fire retardant and stain-proof chemicals, may be harmful to your dog's health.
- **Removable Cover:** If you purchase a dog bed

that has a removable cover it allows for you to regularly and easily clean your dog's bed. Keeping your pet's bedding clean is essential to keeping your pet healthy as it removes bacteria and any parasites that may have found their way into the bedding. Purchasing a bed with a removable cover also allows you to replace the cover if it keeps overly worn and ripped – replacing just the cover is a lot less expensive than replacing an entire bed!

- **Non-Skid Bottom:** When your dog dives into its bed you do not want it to slide across the floor as this could cause damage to your pet, the bed and the floor. Purchasing a bed with a non-skid bottom removes the chance of injury and damages.
- **Plan Ahead:** If you are buying a puppy it is important to remember that your puppy will grow! It is considered best practice to purchase a bed that is the correct size for an adult dog so it will not be out grown.

There are two main categories of beds that are suitable for dogs. It is important to watch your dog sleep so you have an idea of how its sleeping preferences and how it physically lies down. Choosing the correct bedding is vital to ensure your dog feels safe and secure at home. The two categories of bedding are as follows:

- **Round / Nest-Style Beds:** These beds are ideal for smaller dogs and larger dogs who like to curl up when they sleep.
- **Raised / Cushion / Futon Beds:** These beds are ideal for dogs who enjoy stretching themselves out when they sleep.

Food and Water Bowls

It is important to purchase a food bowl and a water bowl for your pet dog. There are three main materials that are used to create these bowls: plastic, ceramic, stainless steel. The following section will outline the pros and cons of each material.

- **Plastic:** Plastic bowls are cheap, durable and long lasting. The only downside of a plastic bowl is that plastic can be toxic to dogs if ingested. If you notice your dog gnawing at its bowl you should replace it with either a ceramic or stainless steel bowl.
- **Ceramic:** Ceramic bowls are very stable and heavy which makes them a good choice if your dog pushes its bowl while it eats or drinks. The main downside of using a ceramic bowl is that they are porous and will

therefore need to be thoroughly cleaned on a daily basis.

- **Stainless Steel:** Stainless Steel bowls are recommended by vets and dog care experts. They are easy to clean, easy to sanitize, durable and inexpensive. Similar to when purchasing a dog bed, it is considered best practice to purchase a stainless steel bowl with a non-skid bottom to prevent the bowl from moving while your dog eats or drinks.

Worms, Ticks and Fleas

Part of your responsibility as a dog owner is to control and kill the parasites that your dog will definitely get at some point. Worms, Ticks and Fleas can cause serious discomfort and health issues if left unchecked. There are medicated collars and shampoos that help to minimize your dog's chance of getting fleas and ticks. There are also medicines you can purchase to help prevent both external and internal parasites. It is considered best practice to take your pet to your local vet and ask for them to give you a prescription for medicines to control parasites.

Toys

Toys for your dog are essential for so many

different reasons! Toys can provide your pet with mental and physical stimulation which can also lead them to having less destructive behavior patterns – such as chewing up furniture! Chew toys can also have dental health benefits. Toys also allow you to build a strong and fun relationship with your pet. The following list details some of the most popular toys available on the market:

- **Chew Toys:** Chew toys can provide your dog with hours of solo fun and can also help your dog to develop a strong and healthy jaw. Before giving your dog a chew toy it is important to check that it is not too hard – an overly hard chew toy can have the opposite effect and damage your dog's jaw! A good rule of thumb is to bang the chew toy on your knee – if it hurts it is too hard for your dog's mouth! It is likewise important to make sure that your dog does not ingest any of the chew toy though as the plastic, or rubber, is toxic!
- **Tug Toys:** Tug toys are a very popular choice as they allow for you to actively play with your dog. It is important to not allow your dog to become aggressive while you play with the tug toy! To avoid your dog becoming aggressive you should keep a positive and

happy inflexion in your voice. The most popular choices for tug toys are ropes and squishy plastic bones.

- **Balls and Fetch Toys:** Balls and fetch toys are another great way to actively play with your pet. It is important to purchase fetch toys made of soft plastic so your dog will suffer no dental damage or physical pain (if they miss the catch and get hit by the toy). A good choice for fetch toys are ball, Frisbees, cuddly toys and squishy plastic sticks. Tennis balls are a common choice for fetch but are not actually a healthy choice of toy! The covering on Tennis balls can actually abrade the enamel on your dog's teeth which can lead to serious health, and dental, issues in later life.
- **Food-Dispensing Toys:** Food-dispensing toys are a great way to mentally stimulate your dog. They come in a variety of different styles and shapes. We recommended purchasing a ball or cube as it will also allow your dog to push the toy around which encourages physical activity as well.

Expanding your Collection

Dogs are incredibly intelligent beings and, like humans, have preferences when it comes to bedding, food and how they have fun. Once you have developed a good understanding of your new dog's preferences we recommended taking these preferences into account when purchasing new equipment and food.

BASIC COST OF OWNING A DOG

Owning a dog obviously costs money – but how much money? The following section will provide you with the average cost of owning a dog to help you decide whether you are in the correct financial state and to help you budget for any unexpected bills! It is important to remember that on average, dogs live for between 8 and 18 years.

Initial costs

- **Purchase of Dog:** Most dog breeds cost between $200 and $1500.
- **Microchip:** If your dog has not been microchipped before purchase this will cost $50.
- **Lifetime Council Registration:** This costs $49 for desexed dogs and $182 for dogs who have not been desexed.

Basic Equipment

- **Dog Bed:** Dog beds normally cost between $20 and $200.
- **Brush:** Most brushes designed for grooming cost around $20.

- **Food and Water bowls:** Each bowl costs are $20 and you will need a minimum of two – one for water and one for food.
- **Collar, Lead, Tags and Harnesses:** A complete set will normally cost between $50 and $200.
- **Toys:** Dogs need a range of toys. We recommend setting aside between $50 and $100 dollars to provide your dog with the enough toys.

Preventative Health Care

- **Vaccination:** Vaccinations cost between $50 and $120 depending on which ones you get. Your dog will need vaccine at 8, 12 and 16 weeks of age and then every 3 years after that.
- **Worm Tablets:** Tapeworm and Heartworm prevention tablets cost about $10 a month.
- **Fleas:** Most flea prevention cost around $10 a month.
- **Bi-annual Vet Check:** You will need to take your dog for a health check at the vet every 6 months. A general health checkup costs around $65.

Food

- **Basic Food Needs:** Basic food (kibble) will cost you around $1,200 a year.
- **Treats:** Treats are not essential but most owners enjoy giving them to their dogs. We recommend budgeting around $100 a year for dog treats.
- **Dental Chew Sticks:** Dental chew sticks are a great way to improve your dog's jaw strength and dental hygiene. We recommend budgeting around $100 a year for dental chew sticks.

Grooming

- **Shampoo and Conditioner:** Shampoo and conditioner will normally cost around $30 a year. It is not necessary to buy expensive brands of shampoo and condition – basic products designed for dogs will work perfectly fine.
- **Visit to the Groomer:** Groomers normally charge between $50 and $150. We recommend taking your dog to the groomers at least twice a year.

Training, Dog Care and Walking

- **Puppy Training:** Puppy training normally costs around $100 for a month long training course.
- **Advanced Training:** Most owners enjoy taking their dogs to obedience classes and advanced training. These services normally cost around $170 for a month long course.
- **Dog Walking:** Dog walking normally costs around $25 an hour (depending on where you live).
- **Daycare:** Daycare services normally cost around $50 a day.
- **Boarding:** We recommend budgeting around $300 a year on boarding services. Most boarding services will charge around $50 a day.

PURCHASING YOUR NEW PET

There are multiple different ways to purchase a dog: from a breeder, from a pet store or from a rescue service. There are pros and cons of each method and they will be explained in the following section.

Breeders

When it comes to purchasing a dog, breeders are unarguably the best method. A breeder will allow you to interact with your dog before you purchase it. This will allow you to understand the dogs temperament and behavior as well as allowing you to inspect the dog for any genetic defects. Breeders are normally a part of a registered service – such as The Kennel Club. By being a member of a registered organization it gives the breeder accountability and legitimacy. Breeders will be able to inform you of any issues with the dog and how they have been socializing it. Breeders will also be able to tell you the exact birthdate of your new dog. The only downside of breeders is the fact that they are more expensive than pet stores – however this should not be an issue when you are considering purchasing a dog.

Pet Stores

Pet stores are a common choice when purchasing a

new dog – but we HIGHLY do not recommend purchasing a dog from a pet store! Most pet stores purchase their dogs from puppy mills. Puppy mills are notorious for breeding and raising their dogs in terrible conditions which leads to both behavioral and health problems. Employees at the pet store will most likely not be able to provide you with specific information about a dog – they are unlikely to know its exact date of birth and health background. The pedigree of a dog from a pet store is also questionable. Pet stores have a terrible return policy! It is not uncommon for a new owner to not have fully considered every aspect of owning a dog and they therefore return it. If you return a dog to a breeder you can be assured that the dog will lead a happy life. However, if you return a dog to a pet store it will most likely be euthanized, if it has grown to be older than a puppy, due to the fact that it is unlikely to sell.

Rescue

If you are an experienced dog owner you may considered getting a dog from a rescue shelter. Most dogs from rescue shelters are free and the shelter just wishes you to make a donation. It is important to remember that rescue dogs may have health or behavioral issues due to their turbulent lives. Dogs in rescue shelters are also hardly ever puppies and tend to be middle aged or older. However by getting your dog from a rescue shelter allows you to give a dog a better life than they would have had in the past. Most dogs that end up in shelters have been cruelly treated or abandoned and by adopting one you are giving the animal a chance to experience life in a loving home.

PUPPY CARE

When purchasing a dog both first time owners and veteran owners normally opt for buying a puppy. Purchasing a puppy will allow you to establish a good and healthy relationship with your dog and will set the foundation for a long happy friendship. Another reason puppies are so popular is due to the fact that they are among some of the most adorable creatures on the planet! However caring for a new puppy is not the easiest thing. You will have to be prepared to make some huge lifestyles changes to accommodate your new puppy. The following section is a simple and concise guide to help you care for the new canine addition to your family.

Find a Good Vet

Before purchasing your puppy it is a good idea to research the vets in your local area. It is very important to find a vet that is local and highly qualified. The best way to find a good vet is by asking your friends, local dog walkers, local dog groomers, asking the breeder and researching online. Once you purchase your new puppy you should take it straight to your vet for a checkup. The checkup visit will make sure that your puppy is in good health and free from any serious birth defects or genetic health issues. Introducing your vet to your new dog while it is young also allows for your puppy to become familiar with the vet – this can help avoid stress during later visits. By taking your puppy to the vet straight away, it also allows you to start a health care routine with your pet. It is important to set up a vaccination plan with your vet and also to discuss the best methods for control parasites (both internal and external).

Food

It is important to purchase food that is formulated specifically for puppies. A decent brand will have a statement from the Association of American Feed Control Officials (AAFCO), or your countries equivalent, on the packaging to ensure that the food you are purchasing is going to fulfil your puppy's nutritional requirements. Small and medium-sized breeds can start eating adult dog food when they are between 9 and 12 months of age. Larger breeds of dog should be fed on puppy kibbles until they reach 2 years of age. It is important to make sure that your puppy has cool, fresh and clean water available to them at all times.

Feeding Schedule

Puppies have a different feeding schedule to adult dogs. Their feeding schedule changes as they get older.

We recommend feeding your puppy on the following schedule:

- **6 – 12 weeks old:** 4 meals per day
- **3 – 6 months old:** 3 meals per day
- **6 – 12 months old:** 2 meals per day

Obedience Training

It is important to train your new puppy to be obedient. Obedience will allow your puppy to have a life full of positive interactions as well as forging a stronger bond between you and your pet. It is important to teach your puppy simple commands such as sit, stay, down and come. These commands will help to keep your dog safe and under control in any potentially dangerous situations. We recommend attending a local obedience training class. Obedience classes allow for you and your dog to learn the best methods for each process and command. Obedience classes also allow you, and your puppy, to interact with other people and dogs of all ages and from all backgrounds. It is important to remember that positive reinforcement has been proven to be a dramatically more effective process than punishment.

Bathroom Training

Housetraining is a priority if you want to keep your

house clean! Before you start your housetraining it is important to locate a suitable location for your puppy to go to the bathroom. If your puppy has not had all of its vaccinations it is important to find a bathroom that is inaccessible to other animals. This will help to avoid your puppy getting any unnecessary viruses or diseases. There are three key tricks to keep in mind when you are attempting to housetrain your puppy: positive reinforcement, planning and patience. It is important positively praise your puppy when they go to the bathroom outside and not to punish them when inevitable accidents will happen. We recommend the following times to try and introduce your puppy to a bathroom routine:

- When you first wake up.
- When your puppy wakes up from any naps it might have.
- During and after physical exercise.
- After your puppy eats or drinks a lot of water.
- Immediately before bed time.

Be Social

The main way to avoid your puppy developing behavioral problems is to be social with it. At approximately 2 to 4 months old, most puppies will begin to accept other animals, people, places and experiences. It is important to start socializing your puppy with as many people and animals as possible. We recommend bringing your puppy to a dog park, to your friends or relatives houses, to dog friendly restaurants and to have other people accompany you while you walk your pet. By interacting with multiple different types of people and animals your puppy will learn to be more social and accepting.

Signs of Illness

It is important to watch your puppy closely to make sure that it is not exhibiting any signs of illness. Your puppy is at its most vulnerable stage of its development while also being at its most important stage of development. If you notice any of the following signs you should take your puppy to the vet immediately: lack of appetite, vomiting, lack of weight gain, lack of growth, diarrhea, pale gums, nasal discharge, inability to pass urine and stool, lethargy, swelling and difficulty breathing.

Spaying and Neutering

There are a lot of factors to considered when deciding if you should spay or neuter your puppy. Many owners refuse to spay or neuter their puppy due to the fact that they find it morally wrong and unnatural. However most owners do decide to have their pet neutered. Shelter euthanasia is the number one killer of dogs and companion animals throughout America. In Atlanta alone over 15 million dollars is spent annually on euthanizing unwanted dogs! The only way to avoid this is to have your pet spayed or neutered. Dogs face some discomfort if they are in heat or are unable to mate. Spaying and neutering creates no long term health problems for your pet. At the end of the day it is an important decision for you and your family to make. We advise talking it over with your vet and family/friends who have already been through the process.

DOG CARE

Once your puppy has grown up, or if you have purchased an adult dog, you will need to change how you care for it.

Dog Food

There are so many different brands of dog food available: organic, all natural, hypo-allergenic, vegetarian and even vegan! Good dog food is vital to provide your pet with the nutrition it needs to reach its full potential both physically and mentally. Good nutrition helps your dog fight disease, prevents obesity, minimizes your dog's chance of getting an illness and generally improves your dog's overall health and happiness. It is important to remember that the advertising on dog food is aimed at humans – because we are the ones that pay for it! You should only feed your dog food that has been approved by the Association of American Feed Control (AAFCO) as it will ensure that the food is both safe and nutritious. You should look for brands of dog food that claim to have an 'AAFCO approved complete and balanced nutritional value' – it is illegal for a brand to claim that they have been approved by the AAFCO if they have not. Make sure the food you purchase contains protein, carbohydrates, fats, vitamins and minerals.

How much to Feed Your Dog

Unfortunately there is no exact method for figuring out exactly how much an individual dog should eat. Determining the correct size meal depends on the type of dog food, how many times a day your dog eats, your dog's size and weight, your dog's metabolic rate, the amount of exercise they get and many other possible variants. Adult dogs are normally fed twice a day. We recommend looking at the feeding guide on the packaging of your dog's food. The feeding guide is normally recommends weights of food based upon your dog's weight. However this feeding guide is not necessarily accurate (your dog may struggle gaining weight or may gain weight at an increased rate). We recommend talking to your vet about how much you should be feeding your dog. It also takes a bit of time to get used to your dog and their eating habits.

Visits to the Vet

It is important to take your dog to the vet on a regular basis. Regular visits to the vet can allow you to treat any issues your dog has in the early stages to avoid them having a negative impact on your dog's health. We recommend scheduling to see your vet at least twice a year – however more frequent visits are advantageous in identifying health problems! It is more important to prevent the onset of disease rather than treat them once they occur. With each visit to the vet you should make sure that you get your dog weighed. By getting your dog weighed on a regular basis you will know if you are feeding it the correct sized portions.

Exercise

Exercise is vitally important to keep your dog happy, healthy and behaving correctly. Dogs, and puppies, have a lot of energy and may develop destructive behaviors if they are not allowed to burn off their energy. How much exercise a dog needs is dependent on its age, breed and health. Most dogs should be walked for at least 30 minutes a day – however we recommend walking your dog for around 60 minutes a day to ensure it has gotten enough exercise. You will know when your dog has had enough exercise when it has slowed its walking speed by a considerable amount. Good exercise uses both physical and mental muscles. We therefore recommend providing your dog with multiple different sources of exercise such as: hiking, walking around your block (using different routines), taking your dog to the park and taking your dog swimming. If you provide your dog with a lack of exercise they are likely to become obese. Obesity in dogs, like in humans, comes with a wide range of health issues. Obesity contributes to a dog developing diabetes, respiratory disease, heart disease and general ill health and tiredness. We recommend living by the following philosophy: a tired dog is a happy, healthy and good dog.

GROOMING

Grooming is an important aspect to caring for your dog! Grooming includes caring for your dog's coat, dental health, nails and over all cleanliness. Dogs enjoy getting messy so sometimes cleaning can be a chore! The following section will highlight all the aspects of grooming that you should consider.

Grooming Tools

- **Bristle Brush:** Bristle brushes are used for all breeds of dog. Bristle brushes help to keep your dog's coat shiny and free from dirt.
- **Clippers and Shedding Blade:** Most species of dog will need to have their coats trimmed in summer to keep them cool. We recommend using clippers for dogs with long coats and shedding blades for short hair dogs.
- **De-Matting Rake:** De-matting rakes have long wire prongs. These prongs are great for removing matts from long coats. It is important to use this tool gently to avoid causing your dog discomfort.
- **Rubber Brush:** Rubber brushes are great for removing dead hair. They create a massaging

effect which many dogs enjoy.

- **Slicker Brush:** Slicker brushes are used to remove tangles and dead hair. They have rows of bent wire pins. They should only be used on dogs with long or thick hair.

Grooming a Long Hair Dog

To groom a long haired dog you should first go over their coat with a slicker brush. Make sure that you are brushing your pet gently to avoid causing any discomfort to your dog as you remove tangles and dead hair. You should brush your dog's legs, tail, thighs, head and back. Once you have gone over the coat with a slicker brush you should then repeat the process with a bristle brush. Make sure to brush in the direction that the coat naturally settles in. The point of the bristle brush is to smooth out the detangled hair. Long haired dogs will need to be brushed on a daily basis. If you want to change the hairstyle of your dog we recommend using clippers. When using clippers it is first important to visualize how you want your dog's coat to look. You should use clippers on your dog's head, feet, legs, sides, underside and body. It is important to trim the fur away from your dog's eyes and muzzle – make sure to take extra care around your pet's eyes!

Grooming a Short Haired Dog

Short haired dogs should be brushed a minimum of once a week. Brushing your dog's coat will stimulate natural oils in their skin and will also remove any dead hair. You should groom your short haired dog by brushing all over its body with a slicker brush. Make sure to start at the head and work your way down. It is important to keep your dog's coat taut as you brush to effectively remove dead hair. Once you have removed all of the dog's dead hair you should brush the dogs coat back into the position it naturally lies in. We recommend using a bristle brush or a rubber brush for this process. You can also comb your dog's coat. A short haired dog will not have excessive tangles in its coat and a fine toothed brush is a perfect way to make your dog's coat look perfect!

Bathing your Dog

Just like people, dogs need a good bathing schedule. Most dogs only require a bath once a month. However if your dog enjoys rolling around in mud and getting especially dirty, you may have to bathe it more often. It is not recommended to bathe your dog more than once a week as it will lose the essential oils present on its skin. It is important to use a dog friendly shampoo and conditioner when bathing your dog as they are designed to not irritate your dog's skin. If your dog has especially sensitive skin it is possible to purchase medicated shampoo to decrease the chance of irritating your dog. We recommend washing your dog in either your bath tub or shower, as it is the least likely to create a watery mess! It is considered best practice to provide your pet with a non-slip mat to keep them secure in the shower or bath tub. Before bathing your dog make sure to have your shampoo and a towel ready to hand. While bathing your pet you should keep one hand on your dog at all times to make sure it does not leave the bath / shower. If your dog is worried about the bathing process reward them with treats to encourage them to relax. You should aim to massage your dog during the shampooing and toweling process to make the bathing experience more pleasurable and fun for them.

Brushing your Dogs Teeth

In America it is estimated that 80% of dogs have some form of dental disease by 3 years of age! Dogs, like humans, need to have their teeth cleaned to remove bacteria and tartar build up. If you do not clean your dog's teeth they are likely to develop Periodontal disease which affects the base of the tooth near the gum line. Dogs can also suffer from dental disease such as gingivitis. It is recommend using a meat flavored toothpaste to reward your dog when it lets you brush its teeth – these toothpastes have the added benefit of being nontoxic if swallowed! You can use a regular toothbrush or a finger brush for the cleaning process. Make sure that the brush has soft bristle to avoid damaging your dog's teeth and gums. Aim to brush each individual tooth for around 5 seconds. It is considered best practice to brush your dog's teeth on a daily basis. Daily cleaning is the best way to prevent dental problems and to keep your dog's breath smelling dramatically better!

Ear Cleaning

Dogs have very long ear canals (around 5 to 10cm in length) that have a right angled bend in them. The bend means that foreign objects can easily get into your dog's ear canal but are very hard to get out! If your dog gets water in its ear, the water can pool at the bend and cause ear infections due to the warm, moist and dark environment of the ear. You should ask your vet how often you should clean your dog's ears, but as a rule of thumb: no more than once a week and no less than once a month. To clean your dog's ears you will need ear cleaner, cotton wool and treats to reward your dog during the potentially uncomfortable process. There are multiple different brands of ear cleaner available and it is important to choose a good quality product. We recommend asking you vet for their suggestion as most pet stores will stock different brands. Once you have the products to hand it is time to start the cleaning process. Gently hold the flap of your dog's ear upright and fill the ear canal with the ear cleaner. It is important to aim the ear cleaner directly downwards as you use it. Once the ear cleaner is in place, massage the skin around your dog's ear to mix the ear cleaner with the contents of your dog's ear canal. Do this for around 20 seconds. Once the massaging time is up, stand up and move away from your dog. Your dog will shake its head vigorously to remove some of the ear cleaner. Once your dog has stopped shaking its head, grab the cotton wool and use it to wipe the folds at the opening of your dog's ear canal until it looks clean. Make sure to reward your dog before and after the ear cleaning process to relax it.

TRAINING

It would seem that dogs enjoy being trained due to the fact that they both enjoy the human interaction of the training process and seem to enjoy 'pleasing' their owners. Training your dog is a perfect way to strengthen the bond between you and your pet as well as being a cool thing to show to non-dog owners.

The Key Components of Training

The following bullet points are the five most important aspects of training any animal:

- Trust
- Positive reinforcement
- Repetition
- Patience
- Consistency

Pre-requisites for successful training

It is vital that your dogs are well socialized and accustomed to both your presence and being handled by you. It is not a good idea to try to train new dogs immediately after purchasing them as they will not trust you and may be frightened or stressed by the training process. Younger dogs, and puppies, are generally more adaptable to training and will therefore pick up new tricks at a faster rate. However younger dogs will also have a shorter attention span which can make the process of training them a long process. Older dogs will have a longer attention span but may be less willing to do physical based training.

Preparation

Before starting to train your dog it is best to know how your dog enjoys spending it's time and what food it loves so you can reward it appropriately. It is important to find one or two healthy treats to reward your dog with to help them stay healthy and motivated during the training process. We recommend rewarding your dog with the following treats: raw carrot, a liver treat or a small piece of chicken. The reason it is important to know your pet dog's preferences is to allow you to work with your pet's natural inclinations and to praise and positively re-enforce the behavior you want.

Clicker Training

Clicker training is considered the easiest and most effective way to train dogs. The concept behind the training is that the clicker tells your dog when they have correctly performed a trick or action. Using a click also allows you to signal to your dog that they have done something correct from a long distance away. Clickers allow you to shape your dog's behavior, which means praising and rewarding closer and closer approximations to the behavior or trick you wish to teach. A click should always be paired with a treat. This allows your dog to create an association between 'clicks' and treats which will encourage your dog to obey clicks. You can purchase a specialized dog training clicker from any pet store or online. Before using the clicker in training, you should pair a click with a reward. Simply click then give your dog a treat. Then wait a few seconds and repeat the process. Repeat this around 10 to 15 times so your dog knows to associate clicks with treats before the training session has even begun.

Teaching Focus and Attention

The fundamental aspect of training a dog is to teach the dog to pay attention to you. You should say the dog's name and then reward them for their attention once they give it to you. Repeat this process several times to ensure that your dog will respond with the appropriate level of attention when you call its name. It is important to shape your dog's behavior through positive reinforcement until you can get your dog to give you full focus – including eye contact.

General Training Tips

The most important training tip is to make sure that you always keep training session short. Short training session will reduce the chance of your dog becoming frustrated and will likewise enhance its concentration. We recommend keeping all training session between 10 and 15 minutes in length. Remember to always reward your dog after clicking to reinforce the likelihood that they will obey clicks. If you are teaching a tricky command, we recommend giving your dog a 'jackpot' of treats when they do the desired trick. By giving your dog more treats than normal will signify that they have done the correct action. It is considered best practice to never end on a failure! If your dog has not fully come to terms with a new trick, you should end the training session by rewarding your pet for completing a trick they already know. This will keep your dog looking forward to training sessions.

Avoid Punishment

Dogs do not learn well by being punished. Punishment will normally make your dog feel confused, stressed and scared – which are not good mental states to be in for learning! A dog that destroys a piece of furniture and looks guilty is responding to your anger rather than knowing what they did was wrong. If your dog is doing something destructive we recommend clapping your hands loudly, or calling its name, to get its attention. Once you have its attention you should lead its focus onto a more productive activity.

What if the training is not working?

It is important that you go into the training process with the intention of having fun and bonding with your pet – any tricks your pet learns will be an added bonus! It is very uncommon for a dog to be untrainable. If the training is not working it is important to think about if you have a close relationship with the dog you are trying to train and if your dog is in the correct mind set to learn tricks. Dogs can easily become bored of repeated training and may likewise be disinterested due to the time of day. Another reason for a dog's disinterest may be that you are offering them the wrong type of treat as a reward. It is important to remember that dogs, like humans, learn at different rates and some dogs will therefore take longer to train. If a dog seems impossible to train it is probably advisable to stop trying to train it and just enjoy playing with it and caring for it.

ILLNESSESS

There are multiple factors that play a huge part on your dog's health: your dog's genetics, the quality of veterinary care they receive, what they eat and how safe the environment they live in is. The following section aims to help you recognize the most common and major threats to your dog's health to allow you to treat and prevent them. Your dog's health is vitally important to giving your dog a chance at a long, happy and healthy life.

Intervertebral Disc Disease (IVDD)

Due to their elongated bodies, Dachshunds are prone to developing back problems. It is therefore important to always support your Dachshunds back while holding it. Symptoms of a back problem include the inability to raise its rear legs, paralysis and the loss of bladder and bowl control. IVDD is treatable if caught early. It is most commonly treated with a surgery that removes the discs that are causing the problems. The best ways to prevent IVDD are to take your dog to an acupuncturist, chiropractor or therapist that has experience in working with dogs.

Epilepsy

Dachshunds have a great chance of having epileptic seizures at some point during their lives. It is unknown why Dachshunds are prove to epilepsy but it is believed to be due to genetics. If you dog suffers from seizures it is considered best practice to take them to the vet as medication can help to prevent epilepsy.

Parasites

Dogs enjoy spending a lot of time outside where they lick and sniff everything, roll around in dirt and puddles and run through long grass. While they find these activities enjoyable they also lead to parasite infestations.

- **Fleas and Ticks:** Fleas and ticks are the most common parasites. Fleas breed incredibly quickly and a couple can turn into an infestation surprisingly quickly. Ticks can cause some very dangerous disease – such as Lyme Disease and Ehrlichoisis. You dog will repeatedly itch itself, either with its paw or against furniture, if it has a tick or flea infestation.
- **Skin Mites:** Skin mites are dramatically smaller than fleas and ticks. Skin mites live

on, or burrow into, your dog's skin and can cause sever discomfort and diseases such as Mange. The main symptoms of skin mites are itching, skin irritation, inflammation and hair loss.

- **Heartworms:** Heartworms are parasites that migrate through your dog's internal system to their hearts and other major organs. Due to the locations they infest, they are extremely dangerous and usually deadly! The most effective way to prevent heartworms is to use a monthly heartworm preventive – medication that can purchased from your vet. There are no symptoms for heartworms other than your dog becoming very ill.
- **Intestinal Worms:** Intestinal worms are very common among puppies. If your dog has recently had a tick or fleas there is a good chance that they now have an intestinal tapeworm. If your dog eats other dog's feces there is also a high chance that they will have an intestinal worm of some sort. The most common way to know if your dog has worms is to physically see the worms in your dog's waste. The best method to keep your dog worm-free is to have a vet perform a fecal test at least once a year.

- **Single Cell Parasites:** Single cell parasites live in your dog's digestive tract. They can cause both Giardia and Coccidiosis if left untreated. If you are giving your dog heartworm preventative medication you normally do not need to worry about single cell parasites as the medication should kill them as well.

Cherry Eye

Cherry eye is a problem that more commonly affects certain breeds but can affect any dog. The main symptom of cherry eye is a large red swelling appearing at the inner corner of one your dog's eye. Cherry eye is caused by the prolapsing of a tear gland attached to your dog's third eyelid. The prolapsed gland swells forward and creates the red bulge. Cherry eye is not a vision threating illness but does cause your dog a lot of discomfort. There are a lot of websites and guides for curing cherry eye at home but we recommend taking your dog to the vet so it receives the best quality medical care from a trained professional. There are two surgical options, performed under general anesthetic, to treat cherry eye. The first is to remove the damaged tear gland completely. The second it to surgically manipulate the gland back into its correct position. We advise that you consult with your vet as to what the best course of action is for your dog's specific case.

Incontinence

Incontinence can affect your dog at any age. If your dog has previously been housetrained, it is important to remember that a loss of bladder, or bowel, control is a physical problem not a behavioral one. Incontinence is most commonly found in older dogs, especially females. Incontinence is normally caused by the following reasons: a urinary tract infection, old age, stress and anxiety, neurological problems (such as seizures), recent spaying surgery, diseases and other health problems. If your dog is suffering from incontinence it is recommend to bring it straight to the vet. The vet will be able to diagnose what is causing the problems and will be able to provide a suitable solution.

Parvovirus

Canine parvovirus is the both highly contagious and most deadly viral disease that affects dogs and puppies. Puppies have an increased chance of catching this illness. Most un-vaccinated dogs who catch parvovirus will die. However, parvovirus is not a fatal illness is identified in its early stages. The best method to prevent parvovirus is to give your puppy, and dog, a full course of medical shots to provide it with strong protection and immunity from the virus. It is also vital to keep your puppy away from other dogs and animals before they have been fully vaccinated! The symptoms for parvovirus are: vomiting, lethargy, a fever and diarrhea. These symptoms are very common for a lot of other less serious illnesses but you should still take your pet to the vet if you notice any as you do not want to risk your dog having untreated parvovirus.

Dental Problems

Most dental problems in dogs are cause by periodontal disease. Periodontal disease can affect more than just your dog's mouth and gums! If your dog has rotten teeth and highly damaged gums they are more likely to catch other illnesses. More dental hygiene can cause your dog to commonly get inflammations throughout their body. The best way to provide your dog with top quality dental care is to provide it with a chew toy. Chew toys allow your dog to strengthen their teeth and jaw as well as removing tartar! There are also multiple different types of doggy dental treats available which are designed to clean your dog's teeth and freshen their breath – Win Win! It is also considered best practice to clean your dog's teeth, either by taking your pet to a professional dental cleaning service, a veterinary clinic or by brush your dog's teeth yourself using a toothbrush. You should strive to make dental care a core part of your dog's grooming routine. The key signs for a dental disease are: excessive drooling, loss of appetite, difficulty eating, broken teeth, loose teeth, inflamed gums, tartar buildup and very pale gums. If you notice any of the above symptoms we recommend taking your dog to the vets.

Ear Problems

The majority of ear problems are relatively easy to treat once they are diagnosed. Ear problems can either be chronic (reoccurring) or acute (one off). Ear infections are one of the most common type of ear problem found in dogs. Ear infections normally occur in the external ear canal and have symptoms of ear redness, scabs and discharge around your dog's ear canal. This type of ear infection is called 'Otitis' and is caused by either a bacterial infection, a yeast or fungal infection, allergies or over exposure to water (such as swimming and bathing). The second most common type of ear problem is an infestation of ear mites. If your dog has ear mites there will be symptoms of black discharge around the ear canal, redness and inflammation of the ear canal, scabbing and a very strong odor. It is best practice to take your dog to the vet if they have any of the above symptoms as the vet will be able to identify the cause of the problem and be able to provide your dog with the best type of medical care. It is considered best practice to not clean your dog's ears before taking them to the vet – your vet will need to see the symptoms of your dog's ear problem. Most ear problems can be corrected through a treatment of oral medication or ear drops.

DANGEROUS FOODS

When owning any pet it is important to know what you should and should not be feeding it. Dogs are no exception to this! There are multiple different foods that can cause sever health problems in dogs – some can even be fatal! Foods that are commonly eaten by humans (both healthy foods and indulgent foods) can be incredibly toxic to dogs. It is important to educate your family and guests on what a dog can and can't eat to avoid someone feeding it something that could damage its health. The following section will outline foods that you should NEVER give to your dog:

Avocado

Avocado leaves, pits, bark and fruit contain a toxin called 'Persin.' While Persin is harmless to humans it has been known to cause breathing difficulties, stomach problems and fluid retention and buildup in the chest. An Avocado's pit is also incredibly dangerous as it will obstruct your dog's gastrointestinal tract if swallowed.

Grapes and Raisins

Both grapes and raisins have been known to cause seriously health problems in dogs – such as liver damage and kidney failure! It is not currently known what specific chemical in grapes and raisins is toxic to dogs. It takes as little as a handful of grapes to seriously poison your dog!

Chocolate

While chocolate is viewed as a treat for humans, it is definitely not for dogs. Chocolate contains a chemical called theobromine which is toxic to dogs. Theobromine will cause a dog to vomit and have diarrhea. It also has the potential to cause seizures and long term damage to your pets nervous system and heart! It is important to watch children around your dog as they may, with the best intentions, feed your dog some of their chocolate.

Coffee and Caffeine

Both coffee and caffeinated products can be fatal if ingested in a high enough quantity. Coffee and caffeine have similar negative effects to chocolate. It causes vomiting, abnormal heart palpitations, seizures and long term damage to the dog's nervous system. It is important to remember that caffeine can be found in a high number of products such as: energy drinks, tea, chocolate, cocoa beans and medicine.

Macadamia Nuts

It can take as little as five macadamia nuts to have a

seriously negative effect on your dog's health. The symptoms of macadamia nut poisoning include muscle tremors, vomiting, rapid breathing, rapid heartrate, increase body temperature and signs of general weakness. If macadamia nuts are mixed with chocolate the combination of poisoning will nearly always be fatal.

Xylitol

Xylitol is a sugar based alcohol that can commonly be found in gum, candy, sweet baked goods and other sugar-substitute items. Xylitol causes no apparent harm to humans but is extremely toxic to dogs. Even a small dose of xylitol can cause seizures, low blood sugar levels, liver failure and even death in dogs!

Yeast

Yeast can be found in basically any dough products (bread, cakes, etc). Yeast will rise and expand in your dog's stomach in a similar manner to how it rises in bread. A small amount of yeast will cause your dog mild discomfort and to be gassy. However if your dog ingests too much yeast it is likely rupture their stomach lining and intestines! It is important to never feed your dog bread or any other products containing yeast.

Onions, Garlic and Chives

It does not matter what form these produces are in (powdered, raw, cooker, dehydrated or mixed with other foods) they are always detrimental to your dog's health. Onions, garlic and chives contain sulfoxides and disulfides which can cause anemia and damage to your dog's red blood cells. Onions, garlic and chives also cause vomiting, breathlessness and general weakness in dogs.

Peaches, Pears and Plums

Peaches contain pits that are potentially a choking hazard to dogs. The pits also contain amygdalin which contains a compound made up of cyanide and sugar that degrades into hydrogen cyanide when metabolized. Hydrogen cyanide is incredibly toxic to dogs and will normally lead to death! Pear seeds contain a small amount of arsenic which is likewise dangerous. Plum pits cannot be digested properly and will therefore cause intestinal obstruction which can cause multiple dangerous health issues. It is important to check your backyard for any trees that produce large fruits and seeds. If you find multiple seeds in your dog's waste it is probably best to cut down and remove the tree.

Cooked Bones

There is a common misconception that all bones are good for dogs. While chewing uncooked bones can help improve the strength of your dog's jaw and provide them with need nutrients, cooked bones are highly dangerous. Cooked bones can easily splinter into sharp, and jagged, pieces. These sharp splinters can tear the lining of your dog's throat or stomach. They will also cause your dog a lot of discomfort as they pass the splintered pieces of bone.

Alcohol

Alcohol has the same effect on a dog's liver and brain as it has on a humans. However the effects of alcohol are greatly amplified on dogs and it therefore takes a lot less alcohol to cause damages – the smaller the dog the greater the effects. A small amount of alcohol can cause vomiting, diarrhea, depression, difficulty breathing, comas and death! Alcohol can obviously be found in beer, liquor and wine but can also been found in some food.

Other Substances to Avoid

The following substances are considered less harmful but should still not be given to your dog:

chewing gum, baby food, apple seeds, corn on the cob, fat trimmings, salmon, tuna, milk and dairy, tobacco, salt, raw meat and raw eggs.

EXTRA THINGS TO CONSIDER

The following sections are extra things to consider that did not fit into any of the above sections.

Vacation

It is likely that you will have a vacation at some point during your dog's life. It is important to remember that not all vacations will accommodate your pet dog. It is therefore best practice to try and line up at least 3 people who would be willing to care for your pet dog while you are away, before even purchasing a dog. Some pet care stores provide a care service for owners while they are on holiday so it is also advisable to ask your local pet store if they offer this service. Another alternative is kennels and boarding services.

Pack Animals

Dogs are pack animals and enjoy being social with humans, other animals and other dogs. If you are going to be away from home for long periods of time (for example at work) it is considered best practice to purchase more than one dog. It is important that your dog does not feel lonely as this will lead to depression and unnecessary stress.

Begging

If your dog begs for food at the table, you are not alone! Begging can seem cute at first but can quickly become an annoying habit. If begging goes unchecked it can escalate into whining during meal times, jumping up onto the table and ever stealing food off plates. The best way to avoid begging is to NEVER allow anyone to feed your dog from the table in the first place. However if you have already fed your dog from the table we recommend ignoring your dog's begging. Once your pet realizes that begging is a futile process they will quickly stop it. Rewarding your dog when it is away from the table, during mealtimes, is the best way to encourage it to stop begging.

Introducing a New Baby to your Dog

Dogs can become jealous. Jealousy can happen in any breed. All breeds, from Rottweilers to Pugs, have been known to bite or attack babies out of pure jealousy. The best way to make sure that your dog does not become jealous is to keep to your established care routine. Do not forget to feed, walk, bathe, train and play with your dog! The first way to introduce your new baby to your dog is to introduce its scent. Bring your dog an item that has your baby's scent on it (such as an item of clothing) and allow your dog to become familiar with the scent. You need to make it clear that your dog needs your permission to sniff the item – this will create clear boundaries and create respect for the baby. Before introducing your dog to the baby it is considered best practice to take your dog for a long walk to drain it of any excess energy. It is important to make sure that the baby, the dog and yourself remain calm during the introduction. Introduce your dog at a distance and over time (weeks) allow it to come closer and closer to the baby. By introducing the baby slowly you are allowing your dog to know that it is worthy of its respect. Most dogs have no issues with new babies! However if you are not 100% confident with the safety of your baby we recommend rehoming your dog. The safety of your baby and dog are the greatest priority (dogs that attack a baby are normally euthanized)!

Location

It is important to consider where you will be living with your new dog. If you are going to be living in a small apartment, or a house without a garden, it may be a good idea to consider purchasing a smaller breed of dog. Likewise, it is important to consider if you neighbors will be bothered by the sound of your dog barking. It may be worthwhile purchasing a breed that is known to be more silent! As a dog owner you will have to ensure that you and your dog have a suitable place to live.

FINAL THOUGHTS

Thank you for purchasing our pet care manual on caring for a Dachshund. We hope you have found the information both interesting and informative. We hope that this book has allowed you to make an informed choice on whether owning a Dachshund suits you and if so we hope that the information will help you to provide the best quality care for your pet Dachshund.

We will be publishing multiple other dog care manuals on our author page on Kindle. If you have an interest in learning more about specific dog breeds then we highly suggest you check out our other work.

Here at Canine Care we are passionate about providing the best quality information to our customers. We would highly appreciate any feedback, or reviews, you could leave us on our Kindle page to allow us to help create the best possible pet care products available on the market.

ABOUT THE AUTHOR

Here at Canine Care we are passionate about dog care. As a brand we have a strong idea of what makes up a good pet care book. We consult with multiple experts in multiple different fields to allow us to create a book filled with cumulative opinions and best practices. The experts we consult range from veterinarians to every day pet keepers who have had years of experience caring for the specific breed each book is on. Our aim, and mission, is to produce the best possible dog care books that are a great value for money.

17399072R00046

Printed in Poland
by Amazon Fulfillment
Poland Sp. z o.o., Wrocław